The Day and Other Poems

ROBERT WELLS was born in Oxford in 1947. He has worked as a woodman, a teacher, in publishing and as a freelance writer and translator. He is married, with two children, and lives in France. He is a Fellow of the Royal Society of Literature.

T0167436

Also by Robert Wells from Carcanet

POETRY
Selected Poems
Lusus

TRANSLATIONS
Virgil, *The Georgics*
Theocritus, *The Idylls*

ROBERT WELLS

The Day
and Other Poems

CARCANET

Acknowledgements

Grateful acknowledgements are made to *The London Magazine, PN Review* and *The Times Literary Supplement*, where some of these poems first appeared.

First published in Great Britain in 2006 by
Carcanet Press Limited
Alliance House
Cross Street
Manchester M2 7AQ

A CIP catalogue record for this book is available from the British Library

ISBN 1 85754 860 4
978 1 85754 860 0

The publisher acknowledges financial assistance from Arts Council England

Typeset in Bembo by XL Publishing Services, Tiverton
Printed and bound in England by SRP Ltd, Exeter

Contents

1

The Forester: Five for S.A.	9
A Memory of Exmoor	12
Ashton	13
The Day	14
At Dusk	18
A Fantasy	18
Meridian	19
Vesperal	19
A Caution	20
New Year	20

2

Antonio	23
Giovanni: Recollections of the Mill	24
Franco	26
Giuseppe	26
Maurizio	27
Adamo	28
Adamo: A Sequel	32
Improvements	32
The Paths	33
The Bathers	33
Monte Gennaro	33
Vintage	34
Broken Weather	34
Hill-Path	35
Meadow	35
Shadowtail	35
Torrent	36
Youth	36

3

Bengal Nights	39
The Cookbook	40
A Blazon	41
To Let	42
Traces	43
The Lake	43
Stressed Syllables	44

The Enjoyment: Two Metaphors   45
Small-Hours Stop   46
Hill-Station Souvenir   47
There   48

                            4

Mr Thewes   51
Old Boy   52
The Thirteenth Book   53
On an Anthologist   54
Moeurs Contemporaines   54
Installation Artists   55
Aspromonte   56
The Fault   56
Bread and Brotherhood   57
The Pillar   58
Portrait of a Virtuoso   61
Palm Leaves   62

Notes   63

1

He knelt, placing his hands
On the stones beside the stream
And bent his face to the water

For the lips
That would not shape themselves to his.

★

'When I looked for myself
I found trees, paths, water, sky, hills.
I found everything that I saw and touched.

These filled me –
There was nothing left of myself.'

★

The elements were hands
That had stripped his body
And went over it, he stood still –

And they felt it as if they were fashioning it
So that no other love could be made.

The Forester
Five for S.A.

1 A Felling

For hard hat, you wore a knitted green cap
To keep woodchips and oil out of your hair.

Poised on its wooden hinge, the enormous beech
Seemed to leap from its base, swung ruinously
Through the air;
                        a slow shock, a long crash –
Branches shattering under their own weight
As the wide canopy folded in on itself,
Continuing to collapse while the trunk lay jammed
Against the gouged-up rubble of the coomb-side.

A shallow root tearing up from where you stood,
You toppled back lightly, chainsaw in hand
– Its blade as long, almost, as you were tall.

2 A Morning Shot

Your rifle club, 'The Outcasts'! Week by week
A score in the high nineties might be remarked
In the sports-page's small print. Your other tally
Went unrecorded.
                        Poacher turned gamekeeper
(On either side, equally clandestine),
You had your cover – a contract forester
Labouring in odd corners – to justify
Your out-of-the-way appearances and errands,
And kept odd hours, the same hours as the deer.

In your outcasts' realm a strict morality
Prevailed. Joke and mischief were its medium,
A picaresque justice the staple of your talk:
How you had the goose off the front lawn of the man
Who paid you short; how, on the day your rivals,

The Hunt, came down, the carcase of a stag
Lay under logs in the back of your parked truck.
– Against its side, binoculars in hand,
Leant some hunt-followers, scanning the long coombs
For the vanished quarry.
                              You had been up early –
Your quiet catchphrase, 'I'll just have a look around.'

3 Below the Moor

Coombs of wrecked oakwood, rhododendron, scree;
An estate's slow overwhelming of itself:

Who would not have been discouraged or have connived
At the settled dereliction?
                              But your energy
Came easily, naturally, as if its source
Lay beyond you in some larger principle
Of activity, drawn on at need by you: a small man,
Only so much of body as might serve
To be the principle's agent.
                              Then no inertia.
The land, as you looked out on it, was tense
With unsprung incident, the deer lying up
On inaccessible slopes. A quickening knowledge
Joined you to what surrounded you, vast views
Of near and far, spacious and intricate;
A field of adventure in which you moved
Secret and cautious, or running like a boy;
Calculating as far as you could, then reckless,
Agilely daring...
                              It was the release of event
Which pleased you, always the participant
Whether as perpetrator or as witness;
Least mere onlooker when most you seemed so.

4 Lumber

Three beechtrunks, trimmed and blunt, awkwardly lying
Aslant the slope, ready to be winched down;
You in a tractor on the drive below:

The noosed cable tightened and jerked, dragging
The first, imprisoned in its own deadweight,
Some heavy yards.
                Suddenly, freakishly,
It rolled, lifted, slid over the smooth bark
Of the trunk beyond it, and jumping lithely clear
Struck the third a huge dull knock broadside.
Then, with lunging slippery momentum,
Skittish almost, as the ground dropped away,
All three together hurtled towards the drive.

From the open cabin came a whoop – long-drawn,
Rising, more shout than cry, more song than shout;
It was your welcome of the incalculable
As the trees bore down.
                They fell in a harmless fork
Around the tractor, to be hauled then to the side
(After a pause of cheerful astonishment),
Laggard, neutralized, to await collection.

5 In Hiding

To accompany the presence and happening
Of things, the light and weather in their changes;
Disqualified by no deranging action,
To make of myself mere consciousness of things
– So to live only in their living through me
And with their entirety to become entire
Was what I aimed at.
                Whether the need to hide
Came first, or sprang from this, I never asked.

If clandestinity gave the common ground
On which we met, yours was of another kind,
Practical, outward. You hid to intervene,
As hungry for the event as I fought shy of it;
Your shot irretrievable, its report and echo
Filling the coomb, splitting the morning's calm,
Dividing before and after by a wound, a death –
The evident trespass you would get away with.

A Memory of Exmoor

On Sundays, walking between the sea and moor
Through derelict woods, up to the dry-stone wall
    That crowned the Sugarloaf,

I'd linger by a gate among hawthorn trees
Encrusted to a grey coral of lichen,
    Where a lost path turned off,

And imagine it the setting for some 'tryst',
The word unreal enough not to beg questions,
    Let alone challenge me

With the clear response cutting through fears and hopes,
That might have come (had someone really been there)
    To test the revery.

Ashton

Trees were suddenly leafless.
Slates on the farmhouse roof
Lay brittler, colder, duller.
Dusted with grit and green
The outhouse sagged more bare
– Frayed boards, putty scaled-off
About each loosening pane.

The heath raised itself up
Darkly beneath a closer
Sky. Sheep coughed in the pen,
Starting to the dash
Of the dog, like grass to wind.
The dog would whimper and cower
For a touch, word or look

To brook a weather
That pried the weakness of trees
– Eponymous grove of ash,
Sentinel beech; and livened
Only the native damps
Of the house, built as it was
Across a hidden stream.

The Day

1

I stand on the doorstep. The land is shadowy,
The sky a red-faint veil – it hardly lights the earth
But is more splendid, more visible than at noon.

They must be wished, the twilit cold and the blank hours.
I gather up chainsaw, fuel, billhook, a small axe
And turn down from the path across the steep hillside.

2

Here the impenetrable wall of fallen trunks,
Saplings, the knit undergrowth of rhododendron
Begins, which day by day I cut back foot by foot.

I rekindle the fire, start the saw, and slowly
My sluggishness changes to a warm ebullience
Which fills my chest as I breathe, and moves in my limbs.

3

Engaged, I give myself to what I see and touch.
This beech coppice, these unmellowing stones, this soil
Are inward events, appearances of a dream

Which matches in everything the world outside me.
To reach that world, to break from the mute trapped turmoil
Of body to an unhindered apprehension!

4

The shrill of the saw, the crash of green, the flaring
Heat of flames surround me, my skin liquid with sweat.
My strength is the obstacle I must break beyond

To attain the clear extreme of water or fire.
I pause, look out unreadily at distant coombs
And the wide Channel; then go more fiercely to work.

5

What I labour to resolve is there as before,
Will not be altered. But moments interrupt me
When, gazing at the broad expanse of land and sea

Bleached into pale colours beneath the winter sun,
My existence ceases to be mine, and becomes
The existence of all things my senses light on.

6

Hunger gains on this unselfed rapture. I break off,
Climb back to eat. What then of the contradiction
Between crass appetite and purged extremity,

The spirit and the human fault? When I return
The trance persists. Like the day it is at its height,
Then like the day it begins to change, to deepen.

7

The moments of effacement become intervals
In which I stand and gaze wherever my eyes fall.
The sea loses its lively brightness, the shadows

That stretched from crannies and branches, interlacing
The afternoon sunlight, fade to make one shadow.
Labour and its relief meet and are of a kind.

8

Dusk. Re-entering my fantasy of struggle
I pile the fire with cut sections of fallen trees,
Wrestle the trunks of rhododendron to the ground.

Earth is already crisping with frost. I touch it
And lift my hand, startled, from the brittle softness.
A dark blue sky, illuminated by the moon.

9

My body has moved every way, is competent
In all its muscles. The impulse of affection?
Giving no sign, it rises still and disperses.

Unbrokenly visible, the loved horizon
Accounted for me. But to be found past nightfall
Staring out at a landscape that cannot be seen...

10

The enchantment vanished, I come back to myself.
Am I the possessor of this flesh, this heartbeat?
Identity has dwindled to a tiny thread

Running through a rough-skinned hand. I gather my tools
And climb back from the hillside to the level path
(Strange to my feet the sudden ease of walking there).

11

I trim and light a lamp, sit over some strong tea,
Lay the fire, light it, wash and eat. Then the evening
Is mine, a clear space in which I can be at rest.

I sit by the fire, unmoving, without feeling.
My senses recompose the landscape and the day –
The horizon bounds me; I lose my body's line.

12

Rested, there is a restiveness that coexists
With this ease and vision. It invades the blank limbs,
A dank stifled undergrowth unreached by the sun.

What expectation has been trapped, what hope disowned?
It is a longing in disguise to be set free,
By shared affection, from this elemental care.

Exmoor, 1971

At Dusk

I tremble at the edge of strength, aware
    What panic lies beyond.
My warmth disperses in the frosty air.
I touch the brittle softness of the ground.

Gathering my tools, some kindling for the hearth,
    I leave the unfinished task
And climb the hillside to the level path,
Its red earth almost colourless in the dusk.

A Fantasy

    A fantasy of battle:
With fire and steel I fight across the ground.
Unfalteringly the sun withdraws. I struggle,
    Running against the bound

    Of warmth and strength, to cram
My fury from the last reserve within.
The moon's cold challenge finds me. Here I am,
    Clear, ready to begin.

Meridian

With a glance I sent myself out to the furthest edge.
The sea, whispering, was my bloodstream.
                                        All there, all one,
A glitter, a certainty, land and sea extended –
Body of the world, to which my senses were given.

Vesperal

It falters in the cold air,
Disperses with the heat of labour;

It has gone, my separate joy,
And cannot be reclaimed

By the effort of memory
Nor shared with another

– A body laid warm
Against the freezing dusk.

A Caution

Look at the land with love, but don't confuse
With your own flesh the field, the path, the hill.

When pressed to serve more than a human use,
Their blankness mocks the effort of your will.

New Year

The cleared hillside paler in the winter's day,
The fire melting now, single, a sobered glare:

The tangle and dead-weight are lifted away;
Stray song of birds ornaments the leafless air.

2

The enigma gone!

Do I care about the despoiling?
— The rape of the riverbed
For gravel,
                    its change
To stagnant shallows,
Reaches of pale mud:

An impure wilderness
Where no way opens
For water or feet;
                         unlearnt
The paths' good sense,
The logic of the streams.

Antonio

Once you had checked your cattle and taken them
To water under the shoulder of the ridge,
You searched around the clumps of broom and bramble
– The ungrazed places – for wild asparagus,
Your brusque hand pushing aside dry briars to pluck
The fine stems that would flavour your midday meal.
Then back to the village by the well-known path
Followed day after day – the broken turf-bank
Swept in May by a flight of yellow orchids,
The sandy defile, more watercourse than track,
The close-paved stretch before the broad loose descent
Into the valley; and between dry-stone walls
Smooth from the riverbed, past orchard, stable,
To your own door.
                            Wouldn't these things sustain you
(Being as much part of you as you of them)
Against the old sickness that came back to dog
Your middle-age: a weak chest, breathing troubles,
A winter that you could not find your way through?
– Since I can see you still, breaking off your search
Across the slope and approaching with a smile,
The bunch of wild asparagus in your hand.

Giovanni
Recollections of the Mill

1

Once the miller had driven off in his trap
To market – he would be away till nightfall –
The boys, waiting and watching at a distance
As the morning's early heat intensified,
Would gather by ones and twos behind the mill
And strip and run out along the *vasca*'s edge:
The walled pool whose collected weight of water,
Coldly brimming, lay idle and unguarded,
Theirs all day long to dive and splash and play in.
Nineteen-sixteen. War was a havoc elsewhere;
Faintly its loud heroics reached the valley –
It could not touch the bathers at their pastime.
Hard now, Giovanni, to think you shared those days,
That trance of quickness and anonymous youth,
Since you so steadily bear so changed a part
In these!
       Resting the mattock against a clod,
You hitch your trousers amply about your waist,
Then, fondly garrulous, push your black hat back
To wipe your forehead and broad grey-stubbled face;
Still working ground in earshot of the millstream
(Your daily bottle of wine laid there to cool).
The stream runs down between briars and willowherb
Across the *vasca*'s silted floor, to vanish,
Gurgling, through metal bars in the far corner.
Mirage of unspent plenty, this other view
Wavers in the warm air between vacant walls.

2

Wartime again. A squad of Germans stationed
In the valley, bored, impatient to be gone –
Their job to guard the road over the mountains
While a retreat continued by other routes.
A young man of the village, a friend of yours,
Stole two oildrums from them. The theft discovered
And the thief known, he ran off into the maze
Of hillside paths and meadows. There he found you.
You stood with him in the high fields debating
– Two innocents, sharing their indecision:
Should he go down? He could hear his family
Calling from below, telling him that the drums
Had been handed back, that he was in the clear.
At last, not thinking that much, if anything,
Would come of it, and hoping to brave it out,
He'd gone back down.
                    The soldiers found and brought him
(Devoted victim for whom their grievance craved)
To an annexe of the mill they'd commandeered.
I had seen it once, though shut up since those days,
A room drearily derelict, with paint-splashed
Discoloured walls and sour dust-coated lumber.
At the far end there was a narrow fireplace
And, built above, a kind of open chimney
Furnished high up with hooks – a handy gibbet.
From this, next day, burnt, beaten and cut about,
His body had been found hanging by the heels.

Franco

The stable at the road's bend (asphalted now,
Once a rubble of white stones);
                                    and you still there,
Calmo, lucente, standing by the doorway
In the early sun, ready with your salute:
A slow good-morning, vowels drawn out as if
There were substance in them to last the whole day

– Though killed in a bike-smash thirty years ago.

Giuseppe

When *rocca stupida*, flaking easily
Beneath our picks, gave way to *rocca viva*,
Its blue-grey crystalline percussion bouncing
The steel back up, we called for you, Giuseppe:
You placed the gleaming wedges, swung the hammer.
So it was, whenever a singular act
Of strength was called for; so it always had been –
Until the arc of the hammer brought you down,
Burst your heart.
                        Yours was the *cruda senectus*
Which Virgil attributes to the Ferryman;
It carried you over quickly to the shades.

Maurizio

1

When you crouched, mallet in hand, on the roof's edge
Whacking at the obdurate rim of concrete
To be broken for the placement of new tiles,
I stood at the apex, protesting, my face
A study in redundant concern,
                                until
You glanced back and good-naturedly silenced me
With your reproach, '*Eh, la pelle è mia!*'

2

'*L'aria è sincera*' –
                      the words spoken
Of the clear dusk, unwittingly of yourself,
As you looked up from the part-dismantled roof
At the sky beyond Lucretilis,
                         to judge
If the tarpaulin should be unrolled that night.

Adamo

1

The road to the village turned back on itself
And leaving the valley-floor climbed round a hill
To planetree-shadowed *piazza*, white stone fountain.
Your makeshift encampment lay down a rough track
Before the turning, and toward the valley's head,
Between the riverbank and a shelving cliff:
A hidden stretch of ground with pens for horses;
Under the cliff, a hardly weathertight shack,
Its fabric patched together out of remnants –
Tufa blocks, odd timbers, corrugated iron.
There your mother lorded it over her tribe
Of indeterminately fathered children
(You were the second) and her summer husband;
Elsewhere, it was said, there were winter quarters,
A winter husband. Watchful and capricious
She seemed to me, incurious, sturdily wild;
Her life a routine scandal, her confinements
The indisposition of two days – the next
She would be up, cutting and carting firewood.
This was your home. When first I went to find you
To fix a day for our proposed crayfishing,
I was dressed up for dancing in the village;
One of your sisters, big-eyed and barefooted,
Tiny in her grubby smock, her nose unwiped,
Stared from beside you and reaching out her hand
Involuntarily, fingered my silk tie
In wonder at the softness, the bright pattern.

2

Ducking beneath its roof of leaves we entered
The riverbed, I following – and waded
Upstream, bent over to scrutinize the pools.
There crayfish hung by ones and twos unmoving
In still grey water out of the main current,
Or stalked invisibly, grey as the water,
Or scooted backward with a flap of the tail
Through a sudden clouding of stirred mud, our hands
Darting to take hold of them as you showed me,
Between finger and thumb, clear of the pincers
Behind the whiskered head, and lift them away,
Tail aflap and pincers impotently stretched
(You held one out, smiling at its vain flourish).
Vigilantly we worked the creeks and shallows,
Wrenched stones over with a crash and rush of sand
Where one might lie in the lee of an eddy
Or find a bolt-hole. Once you surprised a toad
Squatting ominously in its dank hollow
And pelted it with stones (as I would not have);
Once, arm thrust to the elbow in a cranny
Of the bank, you felt a snake gliding away
Under your hand, and started back with a shout,
'*Vipera, vipera!*' The channel narrowed
And steepened among boulders, beneath a scar
Which stood up, grey and orange, into the sun,
Closing the valley. We had a basketful
To be divided, and turned back with our catch.

3

What elements compounded our friendship's fact?
– That pleasant ease in each other's company
Which, given our unlikeness, we hardly knew
What to do with or how to find a shape for.
Your sister's gesture pointed at what we were,
You and I, or were in part to each other:
Characters who had stepped out of a folktale,
As I, in my finery, appeared to her.
Did I waken some hope of a wider world
Beyond the valley, which you might enter on;
A hope that worked as the counterpart to mine
In coming to the valley, for me the place
Where the world opened? Or an erotic hope
Which, if I intuited, I never met
Because I shared it and was afraid of it:
The dreamt-of further signal of affection
Each was unready to ask for, or to give?
Or were you simply, if robustly, lonely,
Shut out, a gipsy, where the village ended,
Because of your parentage and poverty;
The butt of a taboo which I, as stranger,
Knew nothing of, or if I ran against it,
Was unconstrained by? Was it sheer difference
Which proved us brothers, lifting away the bar?
You were fourteen, I seventeen. Together
We stood at a threshold giving upon views
Not then to be teased into identity.

You met me equally, ingenuously
If shyly, holding back out of a courteous
Reserve. And I was hesitant too, in awe
Of the sought-for idol that I found in you:
A presence within the presence of the land,
Summing the land up, self-surrendered to it,
Quickening it through your lively agency.
That was my imposition. And it was true:
You offered the reality of the place
Which made you, body and mind – more palpably
Than if these had been the gift; receiving me
With an archaic decorum, natural
And solemn at once, as prince might welcome prince
Into his borders. But what stays with me now
(My need for such construction having faded)
Varies between the specifics and the myth
In a slighter, nearer, more elusive sense:
However the sun came down the valley-side
To touch the encampment's level ground, it was
The clear obscurity of the riverbed
Which figured your existence, the muted light
Of its low-roofed, winding, leafy corridor –
Chequer of shadow over water and stones;
Your adolescent *vita umbratilis*
Aptly finding a metaphor, a place, there.
I offer what I took from you, Adamo:
These lines must count as my late gift in return.

Adamo
A Sequel

Shouldering your way along the crowded aisle
Until you stand beside me, your face swung close
To mine, as the bus turns into the valley,
You challenge me,
                    '*Ma non mi riconosci?*'
Then, smiling, '*Sono diventato brutto?*'

Don't ask if I recognize you, Adamo.
I know you by the old ingenuousness.

Improvements

Where previously a squalid encampment stood,
Now stands the neat municipal slaughterhouse;

That squatting family gone, their animals,
Their makeshift patchwork of corrugated iron.

Who could object? But everything is tidied,
Or pillaged. Tidiness denies the pillage,

While pillage gives the lie to the tidiness.
Opposite the slaughterhouse, the rubbish dump!

The Paths

Of so much building and passage, what remains?
The ghost of an old patience revivified,

A lost language that looks for a living mouth…
The new-made body – its effort and desire –

Waylaid, abstracted, among coppice and broom,
On cyclamen slopes, beside moss-bearded walls

Where paths run silted with oak-leaves, chestnut husks;
Tacked wire grown into the bark of trees, the wood.

The Bathers

The bathers at their ancient, always renewed,
Never-enough-repeated experiment:

Momentary synthesis of heat and cold
In the integrity of full sensation.

Monte Gennaro

Cut-out marks of a child's toy, the stars hang low.
In the morning the word-giving mountain smiles.

Vintage

Could we set it aside,
    Withdraw our hands
From grape-harvest, the task
    In which we share,

To reach for each other!
    I cannot rest
Merely in your presence
    And my own thoughts.

I look from the vine-leaves
    Where my hands search,
To your face, to the way
    Your body leans,

And then down at the soil,
    Cast where the plough
Has turned it, and crushed mint
    Flavours our steps

Like a wish in common –
    Yes, to lie there
With the dry grit pressing
    Against our skin.

Broken Weather

Ants drown in windfall
Apricots. Through loosened air
The stream sings its waste.

Hill-Path

Crushed rock, torn roots, trickling earth —
The hill-path bulldozed out.
                           I follow it,
A stranger, missing beneath my tread
The old configuration of stones.

Meadow

A smooth meadow. The swallow's low flight there
Accompanies its shadow. Grey amid green,
A heap of stones lies weathering,
Undisturbed since the first clearing of the ground.

Shadowtail

Sudden across the path,
A black squirrel —
Morning's luminous shadow!

Torrent

In hollows of the stream-bed the air lies cool,
Though summer has long dried up the deepest pool.

Here, when late rains and the dog-days briefly met,
Quick bodies would dive and play, brown skin gleam wet.

Youth

Youth, suddenly recollected, means this still:
To watch the weather coming over the hill

And feel, though an unbeliever, dread or love
Raised up in me by a black or smiling Jove.

3

The coin of our pleasure,
Its obverse face
Minted in high relief —

And its reverse?
The same type incuse, stamped
By the punch of taboo.

Bengal Nights

That was 'abuse'.
                    But you were resentful only
When your night-visitors, the eleven cousins
Older than you, drawn to your bed in turn,
Excluded you by day from their licit games.

Alternately the chosen one, the ignored one!
With what bland ease you succumbed, as if by right,
To that importunate cherishing, how gladly
Took instruction from its succession of whims,

I should have guessed, as innocently I played
The role assigned – honorary twelfth cousin,
Your refuge from the others;
                              and have known then
What grievance follows after the charm has failed.

The Cookbook

A great-aunt's parting gift
when you, the pampered youngest
in the household, got your way
and upped and left for England:
a cookbook. You kept it with you
('I couldn't boil an egg')
from that first move, blue clothbound
boards soon stained by use,

its onerous directives
more loosely interpreted
as spices there prescribed
proved unobtainable
and new ingredients beckoned;
– a sibylline vade-mecum,
at last consulted only
fleetingly, for hints.

Heaton Norris, the late
'70s... Our idyll's
bolt-hole. Fondly absorbed,
you'd skin and quarter a chicken
while at your shoulder I'd stare,
illiterate, at the neat
blocks of Bengali script,
projecting on them – what?

Some humanist-imperial
fancy of far-flung truth
which I, by an act of soul,
might recover and translate...
'Pudding', 'Mulligatawny'!
Here and there the text
lapsed for a moment, mock-
heroically, into English.

It was the abstract shape
of print on page – its promise –
that captured me: a blank
which, as I quiz it now,
opens on nights and days
in that sour musty flat
where for a year, occultly,
we dispensed with time and place.

A Blazon

To add an edge to pleasure, I'd startle you
With an account of what you were engaged on,
An obscene blazon whispered into your ear
Accurately phrased.
                  You were more shy of words
Than of what they named. Words netted the dark flow,
Constrained the simple offering of yourself;
Returned you, shocked and charming, to a sudden
Self-consciousness,
              so made you doubly naked.

To Let

It was a mean flat –
you wore your entranced smile,
as if the humble, impossible
requirements of your dream
were answered there
        (humble indeed
beside the huge unauthorized triumph
the dream foretold).

The opaque screen
between your fantasy and the world
had lifted, and in its place
a fragile transparency
lightened your face, taking away
the enclosed look
in your large eyes.

★

Communal, desolate, the hallway
– its payphone and loose tiles –
was lit through the porch's parti-coloured
glass (some lozenges missing). Privet
bushed out into the unmade road,
the unmown garden.
               We
took courage from neglect.

Where softened Victorian brick had once
proclaimed a home a castle,
we were the squatting heirs, come back
anonymously, glad of a nook
to lodge
        our unhistorical joys.

Traces

The smile of the unrecorded –
to catch that was the mischievous
promise you held out,
the lure which drew me on.

Your dance threw off a foam
of movement, which dissolved
invisibly about you,
a trace felt in the moment

that it evaporated...
A boat's wake closing over,
a shooting star's brief track:
these were your metaphors.

Now this:
         darling and scapegoat,
you flourished, as if secure,
in the temporary shelter
commandeered by your charm.

The Lake

Love was the dark lake in which we bathed together.
I stand on the bank now. You are drowning out there.

Stressed Syllables

For you the erotic was barely
involved with words (as it was
– intimately so – for me).

You preferred hints, teasings,
smiling periphrases,
sly clickings of the tongue.

Only *in extremis*
would you try ordinary terms,
as on the occasion when,

face down, with a small gasp,
complicit in subjection,
you murmured 'circumcised...'

– secret obsolete badge
of empire, sported by us
in our renegado game;

the two stressed syllables
timed to the two strokes
that quickened me to orgasm.

The Enjoyment
Two Metaphors

1

You wriggled to evade; preliminary hurt
Welled into pleasure and you gave yourself up,

Arms and legs spreadeagled – beams of a star
Struck through its centre, bright resistance gone,

And the enjoyment, bearing you darkly onward,
Passed into nonentity (this, too, desired).

2

What smiling reaches the circuitous path
Led us through: high woodland, dew-matted lawns,

Waters to drink at and return to drink at!
We knew that we would emerge below the crest;

We would climb the mountain of our *jouissance*
And stand above it amid vertiginous skies.

Small-Hours Stop

As with the remembered journey, so with love:
We too travelled the ancient route, transformed
Its incidents into emblems.
                              For example,
Our small-hours stop in that small silent town,
A staging-post between the plain and mountains.
Huddled among the crowd of passengers,
We sipped thick tea at a charwallah's stall
While the night-bus, its engine idling, waited;
Each of us cradling in a hand the rough
Earthenware cup, glad of its inch of sweetness
And eyeing the fire beneath the pot.
                                   Refreshed,
I strolled aside. Along the shuttered highway
The ground crunched softly, unevenly, underfoot
And, glancing down, I made out in the shadow
How, for some distance round, greyly apparent,
The place was paved and mounded with a vast
Detritus, where cup on cup had been let fall
To be trodden back to earth,
                            as in a moment
Ours would be (the bus honking its summons),
Our passage counted with the countless others.

Hill-Station Souvenir

From shrouded vantage-point to vantage-point
The guide conducted us that fogbound morning,
Promising us the views that might have been.
We stared politely into the wall of grey,
Soft and unvarying. Finally he brought us
To a small terrace above a hidden gulf
From which we should have seen a facing cliff
(He gestured grandly) plunge sheer to the plain.
It was no day for the sublime. We waited,
Mist catching in our throats, curling in our faces,
In case the cloud should thin, and a stone edge
Show like a shadow – then filed back again,
You and I with the others.
                     At the entrance
Some vendors of eucalyptus oil stood ready,
Bottles set out on the instant. One, to prove
The purity, dipped a rag in the oil
And set light to it, then (having let it flare)
Pinched out the flame, leaving the rag unsinged.
We bought a bottle. I, without conviction,
Tried it that night on an ankle dully sprained
And woke to find the ache abruptly gone.
But that slight comedy of surprise is hardly
What saves the incident for me.
                         It was the flame,
Bright, quick, open, contrary, loose, free,
Coming as if out of nothing, richly fed,
Welcome and warm, which startled me, and stays.
How it burned back vagueness and opacity!
– An image of the desire that was between us
Certainly; but the desire itself
A further recession within the metaphor,
Figuring the half-forgotten, the unimagined:
As we had seen, struck from its latent source
In watery diffusion, the gush of fire.

There

There the secret is shown, the unspoken spoken,
The hidden grief rejoiced in, the worry over.

There, of taboos, you will at last discover
That the most rigid may be the soonest broken.

There an old difference changes to a token
Of likeness – forcing you, high-minded lover,

Down from the cloudy reach where wishes hover,
Your pleasure focused now, your need awoken.

One day each summer I would come home from school
To find our alley newly stripped of its green,
Wild ragwort gone from crannies under the wall,
Neat cobblestones with no moss or grass between.

Moss, grass and weeds would gradually grow back
And the year make good what had been cut away.
But, naked, the alley wore a shamefaced look
Which touched me as if the want were mine that day.

Mr Thewes

for Fernand Benhaiem

The Jewish lawyer from Constantine and I
Sit in a Blésois café, in bland exile,
Over morning coffee, as he recollects
His English *prof* at the Lycée, Mr Thewes,
The first foreigner whom he had ever met:
How good-natured he was; an outsider, both
Where République and Rabbinate were concerned,
The settled proprieties of school and home
Suspended in his lessons; how his story
(To teach the risks of mispronunciation)
About the finical lady who confused
'Je me lave le cou' with *'Je me lave le cul'*
Delighted the class – he had *'l'esprit Gaulois'*;
And how he would caress affectionately
The curls of the ill-fed, unprepossessing,
Excitable boy, winning him on to learn.
'Il était sensible à ma pauvreté…'
'Il a vu que j'étais un bon élément…'

War came and with it a new term. In class now
No Mr Thewes. Then the word came he was dead,
Killed, how and where not reported, a young man
Not twenty-six yet. Three months later the boy
– Excluded (*'On ne peut pas, il est doué…'*)
From the Lycée, under Vichy – had gone too,
Not understanding either loss, but sensing
That they must be connected. Sixty years on,
Mr Thewes is recalled *'avec peine'*, the words
Heavily spoken and repeated, the grief
Fresh in my friend's face; with a grateful fondness
Both for the man and an imagined England,
Suggested to the boy by his courtesy
And kind regard. His memory, pushing up
Against the odds – I think, like the one grassblade
Through asphalt, noticed by me in the pavement
As we pay and leave –, greenly raises itself
To show in our conversation and these lines.

Old Boy

Your name under *Deaths*
in the Old Boys' Newsletter –
last seen when we were twelve!
Precocious then as now,

you were first among us
to have reached and crossed
the sill of puberty.
We were impressed,

in the changing-room,
by your shadowed nudity,
the sex heavy-hung
in its thicket of hair

– too grave a sequel
for our jokes to master,
much less disown;
since, late or early,

shamefaced or immodest,
which of us was exempt?
Decently unabashed,
you merely showed the way.

No time. A lifetime.
The random image
of your fresh ripeness
(perfectly retained)

finds its place now,
clear of intervening
vicissitude, beside
this bare announcement.

The Thirteenth Book

When pious Aeneas got fetched up to heaven,
It was not a moment too soon. He had grown sick
Of his household gods with their incessant demands.
After the years of trouble to find them a home
Why couldn't they sit on the proper shelf in peace,
Not jostle angrily there, invoking the fates
And calling out (spoilt brats) for further sacrifice?
There would be no more rising to the occasion.
That final combat had taken it out of him!
Had no one stopped to reflect amid the applause,
As Turnus's indignant spirit sought the shades
And he lightheadedly pulled his sword from the corpse,
That he too was done for, the epic at an end?
For half his life it had served as his hiding-place,
A factitious destiny he'd gladly shouldered
Like a suit of armour, shielded within his role.
Who was he? No one had ever needed to ask.
He was pious Aeneas, heavily engaged
In the business of piety, and if that made
For a certain blankness, well what could you expect?
He felt his age now. Even the long-counted-on
Desire to cut loose was weaker than he'd supposed.
Yet, loitering facelessly about the palace,
He recalled certain landfalls with crushing regret,
The time at Carthage (that time in the stormlit cave),
And not Dido only but other instances
Too slight for the record, the curve of a veiled hip,
A smile out of shadow, a path leading away
Under palms or pines, dusty inconsequent track
To the untried life beyond omen or taboo…
Meanwhile he had become an encumbrance merely,
Ineffectual, daydream-sodden, a figurehead
Lolling aphasic, as life went on despite him
– Since there was a country to govern, after all;
(The past must not be allowed to get in the way).

Fidus Achates came to an understanding
With Queen Lavinia, who had motives of her own.
They smothered him with a pillow as he lay drunk
And dropped his body, weighed with stones, in the Tiber,
Then put out their story of apotheosis
And called in another poet, more biddable
Than the previous one, to fake up a thirteenth book.

On an Anthologist

It does good to body and soul
When I open my fly, take aim
(Looking down at the lavatory bowl)
And piss all over your name.

Moeurs Contemporaines

'The first adult decision of my life,'
Said the young poet
Who had just walked out on his wife and 'kids'.

Installation Artists

1990s

1

Aesthete, puritan,
his bad conscience
gave him a nose for the main chance.

2

A practitioner
of the new genre,
in-your-face obliquity.

3

At the century's end
a Modernist,
vaunting his blowzy rigour.

4

Ass's ears!
and yet how circumspectly
the turban is adjusted.

Aspromonte

A dry riverbed. Stumbling across
its sprawl of boulders, he does not guess
at the water that still runs beneath.

But he is near the sea. The first hills
go up on either side, steep orchards
with unripe plums, slopes of coppice oak,

a line of distant crests. From habit,
he forces himself on through the heat.
He does not guess what upland coolness

is there to meet him among big trees –
the air a live presence about him,
the water pushing through his dipped hand.

The Fault

What Youth had cherished was the body's neatness,
    A separate competence to set against
The soul-defeating sense of incompleteness
    By which a deeper fault was evidenced.

Bread and Brotherhood

in Luristan

He came out of the house with bread in his hand.
His mother had just baked it, as he told me
(I happened to be walking by); and, tearing
Half the strip off, he offered it with a smile,
The flat uneven *nan*, mottled with scorch-marks,
Still warm and moist in its first freshness.

We stood

In the dusty track before his curtained door,
Munching companionably and looking out
At the morning and the land, the nearby spring,
The grove it watered, acres of corn and beans,
Then arid pasture with clusters of black tents:
Encampments of village families, for whom
– A generation's stone-throw from nomadism –
The habit of mud walls and poplar rafters
Proved hard in summer, in spite of planted fields.

Off to one side and out of view, the *tepe*:
Our excavation all but finished, the mound
Of habitations sifted now, dug-down-through
Past layers of burning, resettlement, neglect,
To the first ground-plan, the original floor,
Its beaten earth uncovered and newly swept…
I'd stretched out there as if to claim possession.

His name was Karim.

True, we liked each other

Though hardly in a way that had been tested
Beyond good nature's limit; were the same age,
Had shared a season's labour. But that meeting
– Call it the moment of bread and brotherhood –
Comes back persistently across thirty years
In its first freshness; not as more than itself,
If vivid, scarcely a parable – and yet
The sum of what can humanly be hoped for.

The Pillar

In the Temple of the Holy Sepulchre,
Along a shadowed aisle, there stands a pillar
　　Marked from head-height to floor
With little crosses, irregularly neat –

A host of them, each carved by a crusader
To witness his arrival, his vow maintained;
　　For so much risk and road
No blazon beyond this anonymous sign.

Running my hand over the polished surface
As if to gather up a swath of journeys,
　　I felt the crosses' edge
Under my palm and fingers, an enigma

Coolly unyielding. With this came the desire
To reach behind the emblem, along each route
　　From pillar to homeground;
So to recover the content of the voyage.

★

I had forgotten. Disgust shadows desire.
Another life is never safely envied.
　　The knowledge once attained,
We shy away from what we needed to know.

A hair's-breadth separates the panegyric
From an art that seals in words what can't be borne,
　　So that it won't come back;
Neutralized its capacity to distress.

This holding true of holidays and heroes
(As, how much more, of the plight of every day),
　　What then of desperate souls
Cursed by deeds they had acted, suffered, witnessed?

How could I quarrel with the instinct to close
The journey off behind the destination?
     But, pressing these thoughts down,
My jealous admiration was what prevailed.

★

The old recourse: imagination's compound
Of memory and wish. To make the fiction,
     I turned on my own tracks,
Conjured the darkling shift of harbour waters

On late eves of departure, morning seascapes
A-glitter, glimpsed unvisited Cytheras,
     Shoaled landfalls, rounded capes;
Tawny deserts, colour of a lion's pelt,

Forests, lakes, rivers, marshes; cliff-hung passes,
Thin upland reaches, green becalmed expanses,
     Broad highways, breakneck paths;
Hill-huddled villages, plain-circled cities,

Far mountains, pale at midday, purple at dusk;
Skies crazed by lightning, rain-riddled, dull with snow,
     Tyrannized by the sun:
The gamut of weathers over land and sea.

★

What bivouacs, embarkations, bargainings
For passage, what fevers and recoveries,
     What respites and fatigues,
Incised and hidden here, might have been evoked

To witness the dizzy sum of pilgrimage?
Idleness under awnings, the creak of oars,
     Water lapping worked stone,
Dolphin-outriders crossing before the prow

As it lifts and dips amid the swing of waves;
On a rainy morning in some market-place
   A cup of sweetened milk,
A cake, and from the vendor, muzzy with sleep,

A young gratuitous smile; trust and distrust;
Promiscuities of bed and board and road;
   The one assured treasure
A life, in recollection, truly possessed.

★

'The past', I said, 'lives in us or not at all,
As, stumbling on its exclusions, we are forced,
   Each opening instant, out –
But out into a future cognate with it

And to be turned to as a source of knowledge
Which can make good the exclusions.' This once said,
   I felt my envy wane:
The slow accretion of crosses notched in stone

Stood in no contradiction with the instant;
Was itself alive with possibility,
   Fixed there as if in flight
And beautiful in its fortuitous shape.

I thought of birds taking off at a handclap
Or cracked stick, from a tide-washed river-island,
   Wheeling and scattering,
The great flood and the bright air spaciously theirs.

Portrait of a Virtuoso

Coins, potsherds, fossils: always need and hope of
Discovery, design in little.
                              Looking
Was a half-life; finding meant full existence
(But that existence self-enclosed, unspoken,
One secret more among the household secrets)
For the timid virtuoso, twelve years old,
Who stares out searchingly from the photograph.

He has a claim upon me, and within me,
Which I can neither answer nor put aside.
Who is reaching to whom for what kind of help
Which can't be offered?
                              Yet there is common ground
On which to meet: the talismanic value
Assigned to certain objects, recollected
As vividly as if they lay in my palm,
Or I were standing beside that appletree,
Now long cut down, a hand on its scaly bark...

Curled *Gryphaea*, the lesser valve still intact,
Hinged in concave embrace to the outer shell,
'The Devil's Toenail'; an orange aurochs-tooth,
Broken-rooted, from Tertiary gravel;
Struck from its clayey nodule, an ammonite –
The ribbed circuits and mossy-patterned sutures
Of the shallow vortex perfectly exposed;
A flint scraper; a polished basalt axehead;
The black rim of a Tuscan pitcher, printed
With shapely roundels; an earthenware loom-weight;
An *as* of Vespasian, the patina'd face
Pitted by volcanic ash; a charred fragment
Of planking from a Roman galley:
                              items
From his cabinet of curiosities;
Each trophy labelled and set out on display,
A sop to reticence, an oblique challenge,
A wooing of the wide world of time and place.

No wonder that, despite his uncertain gift,
Poetry should have set an ambush for him
At the next turning.
                    What was it ran beneath
Such mixed anxiety and expectation,
If not compulsive longing for an enforced
Openness, by which things might be named and shown?

Palm Leaves

Moulded in white plaster
on the chapel wall,

palm leaves – now no longer
martyrdom's symbol,

thank god, but as themselves
the more beautiful!